EMMANUEL JOSEPH

The Ethical Wardrobe, How Fashion Can Save the Planet and Our Conscience

Copyright © 2025 by Emmanuel Joseph

All rights reserved. No part of this publication may be reproduced, stored or transmitted in any form or by any means, electronic, mechanical, photocopying, recording, scanning, or otherwise without written permission from the publisher. It is illegal to copy this book, post it to a website, or distribute it by any other means without permission.

First edition

*This book was professionally typeset on Reedsy.
Find out more at reedsy.com*

Contents

1	Chapter 1: The Fast Fashion Frenzy	1
2	Chapter 2: The True Cost of Fashion	3
3	Chapter 3: The Rise of Ethical Fashion	5
4	Chapter 4: The Power of Consumer Choice	7
5	Chapter 5: The Role of Technology in Sustainable Fashion	9
6	Chapter 6: The Slow Fashion Movement	11
7	Chapter 7: The Environmental Impact of Fashion	13
8	Chapter 8: The Social Impact of Fashion	15
9	Chapter 9: The Intersection of Fashion and Culture	17
10	Chapter 10: The Future of Sustainable Fashion	19
11	Chapter 11: The Role of Policy and Regulation	21
12	Chapter 12: The Ethical Consumer	23
13	Chapter 13: The Impact of COVID-19 on the Fashion Industry	25
14	Chapter 14: The Role of Education in Sustainable Fashion	27
15	Chapter 15: The Influence of Social Media on Fashion	29
16	Chapter 16: Building a Sustainable Fashion Brand	31
17	Chapter 17: The Journey Towards an Ethical Wardrobe	33

1

Chapter 1: The Fast Fashion Frenzy

Fast fashion has taken the world by storm, transforming how we buy and consume clothing. Brands churn out new collections at breakneck speed, enticing consumers with trendy, affordable pieces. However, behind this seemingly glamorous façade lies a darker reality. The rapid production cycle encourages a throwaway culture, where garments are worn only a handful of times before being discarded. This relentless pursuit of the latest styles has dire consequences for both the environment and the workers who produce these clothes.

The environmental impact of fast fashion is staggering. The industry is one of the largest polluters globally, contributing to massive water consumption, chemical pollution, and textile waste. The production of synthetic fibers like polyester releases microplastics into water bodies, which eventually make their way into the food chain, affecting marine life and human health. Moreover, the energy-intensive processes involved in textile manufacturing contribute significantly to greenhouse gas emissions, exacerbating climate change. As consumers, we must recognize the true cost of our fashion choices and shift towards more sustainable practices.

The human cost of fast fashion is equally alarming. Garment workers in developing countries often endure exploitative working conditions, long hours, and meager wages. The Rana Plaza disaster in 2013, which claimed the lives of over 1,100 workers in Bangladesh, brought the harsh realities of the industry to the forefront. Despite global outrage, many brands continue to prioritize profit over people, neglecting the well-being of their labor force. Ethical fashion advocates argue that we must demand greater transparency and accountability from brands, ensuring fair treatment and safe working conditions for all workers.

As consumers, we hold the power to drive change within the fashion industry. By making more informed choices and supporting ethical brands, we can contribute to a more sustainable and just fashion ecosystem. Opting for quality over quantity, embracing second-hand shopping, and extending the life of our garments through proper care are just a few ways we can reduce our fashion footprint. Ultimately, our collective actions can help create a world where fashion is a force for good, benefiting both the planet and its inhabitants.

2

Chapter 2: The True Cost of Fashion

When we pick up a trendy shirt for a few dollars, we rarely consider the true cost behind the price tag. The fashion industry is notorious for its exploitative practices, which often include underpaid labor, poor working conditions, and environmental degradation. The relentless drive for profit and the constant demand for new products have created a cycle that is unsustainable and harmful.

The human cost of fashion cannot be overstated. Garment workers, mostly women in developing countries, often face long hours, low wages, and unsafe working conditions. These workers are the backbone of the fast fashion industry, yet they are often the most marginalized and vulnerable. The Rana Plaza tragedy in Bangladesh is a stark reminder of the industry's failures, where over 1,100 workers lost their lives due to poor safety standards. This incident brought global attention to the plight of garment workers and the urgent need for reform.

Environmental degradation is another significant cost of fast fashion. The industry is responsible for massive water usage, chemical pollution, and textile waste. The production of cotton, a common fabric, requires vast amounts of water and pesticides, leading to soil degradation and water scarcity. Synthetic fibers, such as polyester, contribute to microplastic pollution, which has far-reaching effects on marine ecosystems and human health. The carbon footprint of the fashion industry is also immense, with greenhouse gas emissions from production and transportation contributing to climate change.

As consumers, we have the power to drive change by making more conscious choices. By supporting ethical brands, buying second-hand, and prioritizing quality over quantity, we can reduce the demand for fast fashion and its harmful practices. Additionally, advocating for better labor rights and environmental standards in the industry can help create a more sustainable and equitable fashion landscape.

3

Chapter 3: The Rise of Ethical Fashion

In recent years, there has been a growing movement towards ethical fashion, driven by consumer demand for more sustainable and humane practices. Ethical fashion encompasses a range of practices, from fair trade and organic materials to cruelty-free production and circular fashion. This movement aims to address the negative impacts of the fashion industry and promote a more responsible and compassionate approach to clothing.

Fair trade is a key component of ethical fashion, ensuring that garment workers receive fair wages and work in safe conditions. Fair trade certifications provide consumers with the assurance that their purchases support equitable labor practices and contribute to the well-being of workers. Brands that prioritize fair trade often work closely with artisans and communities, fostering long-term relationships and sustainable development.

Organic materials are another important aspect of ethical fashion. Organic cotton, for example, is grown without harmful pesticides and requires less water than conventional cotton. This reduces the environmental impact of production and promotes healthier ecosystems. Other sustainable materials, such as bamboo, hemp, and recycled fibers, offer eco-friendly alternatives to conventional textiles. By choosing garments made from organic and sustainable materials, consumers can support practices that protect the environment and promote biodiversity.

Circular fashion is an innovative approach to reducing waste in the fashion industry. This concept involves designing products with longevity in mind, encouraging repair, reuse, and recycling. Brands that embrace circular fashion create durable garments that can be easily repaired or repurposed, extending their lifecycle and reducing the need for new resources. This shift towards a circular economy in fashion challenges the traditional linear model of production and consumption, promoting a more sustainable and regenerative system.

The rise of ethical fashion reflects a growing awareness of the interconnectedness of our choices and their impact on people and the planet. As consumers become more informed and conscious, the demand for ethical fashion continues to grow, driving positive change in the industry.

4

Chapter 4: The Power of Consumer Choice

Consumer choice is a powerful tool for driving change in the fashion industry. As individuals, we have the ability to influence brands and shape market trends through our purchasing decisions. By prioritizing ethical and sustainable fashion, we can create a ripple effect that encourages more brands to adopt responsible practices and fosters a culture of accountability.

One way to make more ethical choices is by supporting brands that prioritize transparency and sustainability. Many ethical fashion brands provide detailed information about their sourcing, production processes, and labor practices, allowing consumers to make informed decisions. By choosing to support these brands, we can help create a market that values ethical practices and encourages others to follow suit.

Second-hand shopping is another effective way to reduce the environmental impact of our fashion choices. Thrift stores, consignment shops, and online marketplaces offer a treasure trove of pre-loved garments that are often of high quality and unique style. By giving clothing a second life, we can reduce the demand for new products and the associated resource consumption and waste. Additionally, second-hand shopping often supports local businesses and charities, creating positive social impacts.

Another important aspect of ethical fashion is extending the life of our garments. Proper care, such as gentle washing, mending, and storing, can significantly increase the lifespan of our clothes. By treating our garments with care and respect, we can reduce the frequency of replacement and minimize our fashion footprint. Additionally, learning basic sewing skills and embracing DIY fashion can empower us to repair and customize our clothing, adding a personal touch and prolonging its usability.

Ultimately, the power of consumer choice lies in our collective actions. By making more conscious decisions and advocating for ethical practices, we can drive meaningful change in the fashion industry. Our choices can inspire others, create demand for sustainable products, and contribute to a more just and compassionate world.

5

Chapter 5: The Role of Technology in Sustainable Fashion

Technology plays a crucial role in advancing sustainable fashion practices and addressing the environmental and social challenges of the industry. From innovative materials and production methods to digital platforms and supply chain transparency, technology offers numerous solutions for creating a more ethical and sustainable fashion ecosystem.

One of the most exciting developments in sustainable fashion is the use of innovative materials. Biofabrication, for example, involves growing textiles from living organisms, such as bacteria, yeast, and algae. These materials are biodegradable, reducing the environmental impact of clothing disposal. Additionally, biofabricated textiles often require fewer resources and chemicals during production, making them a more eco-friendly alternative to conventional fabrics.

Another technological advancement is the use of 3D printing in fashion design and production. 3D printing allows for precise and efficient manufacturing, reducing waste and resource consumption. Designers can create intricate and customized garments with minimal material waste, and production can be localized, reducing transportation emissions. 3D printing also offers the potential for on-demand manufacturing, eliminating excess inventory and promoting a more sustainable supply chain.

Digital platforms and tools are also transforming the fashion industry by promoting transparency and accountability. Blockchain technology, for example, enables secure and transparent tracking of products throughout the supply chain. This allows consumers to verify the origins and ethical practices of their garments, fostering trust and informed decision-making. Digital platforms can also connect consumers with ethical brands, second-hand marketplaces, and clothing rental services, making it easier to access and support sustainable fashion options.

Additionally, technology can enhance the efficiency and sustainability of production processes. Innovations in dyeing techniques, for example, can significantly reduce water and chemical usage. Digital printing and zero-waste pattern making are other methods that minimize waste and resource consumption. By adopting these advanced technologies, the fashion industry can reduce its environmental footprint and promote more responsible production practices.

Technology's role in sustainable fashion is continually evolving, offering new opportunities to address the industry's challenges. By embracing and investing in innovative solutions, we can pave the way for a more sustainable and ethical fashion future.

6

Chapter 6: The Slow Fashion Movement

Slow fashion is a response to the fast fashion frenzy, emphasizing quality, longevity, and mindfulness in clothing choices. Unlike fast fashion, which prioritizes rapid production and consumption, slow fashion advocates for a more deliberate and thoughtful approach to fashion. This movement encourages consumers to invest in well-made, timeless pieces that can be cherished and worn for years.

One of the core principles of slow fashion is to buy less and choose well. This means prioritizing quality over quantity and selecting garments that are made to last. High-quality materials and craftsmanship ensure that clothing can withstand wear and tear, reducing the need for frequent replacements. By investing in durable pieces, consumers can build a versatile and sustainable wardrobe that stands the test of time.

Another aspect of slow fashion is embracing a minimalist mindset. This involves curating a wardrobe with fewer items that are versatile and can be mixed and matched. A minimalist wardrobe focuses on essential pieces that reflect personal style and can be worn in various combinations. This approach not only reduces clutter but also encourages mindful consumption and a deeper appreciation for each garment.

Supporting local and independent designers is also an important element of slow fashion. These designers often prioritize ethical and sustainable practices, creating unique and high-quality pieces. By supporting small businesses, consumers can contribute to a more diverse and resilient fashion ecosystem. Additionally, local production reduces the environmental impact of transportation and promotes community development.

The slow fashion movement encourages us to rethink our relationship with clothing and adopt a more conscious and sustainable approach. By valuing quality, embracing minimalism, and supporting ethical designers, we can create a more meaningful and enduring wardrobe.

7

Chapter 7: The Environmental Impact of Fashion

The environmental impact of the fashion industry is vast and multifaceted. From resource extraction and production processes to waste generation and pollution, the industry's practices have far-reaching consequences for the planet. Understanding these impacts is crucial for driving change and promoting more sustainable fashion practices.

One of the most significant environmental challenges in fashion is water usage. The production of cotton, a common textile, requires enormous amounts of water. In some regions, this has led to water scarcity and competition with local communities for essential resources. Additionally, the dyeing and finishing processes in textile manufacturing consume vast quantities of water and often result in the discharge of toxic chemicals into waterways, harming aquatic ecosystems and human health.

Chemical pollution is another major concern. The fashion industry relies heavily on synthetic dyes, finishes, and treatments that can be harmful to both the environment and workers. These chemicals can contaminate soil and water, posing risks to wildlife and human populations. The production of synthetic fibers, such as polyester, also involves the use of petrochemicals and releases microplastics into the environment. These microplastics can persist for centuries, accumulating in oceans and affecting marine life.

Textile waste is a growing problem, with millions of tons of clothing ending up in landfills each year. The fast fashion model encourages a throwaway culture, where garments are quickly discarded once they go out of style or become damaged. This waste not only takes up valuable landfill space but also releases greenhouse gases as it decomposes. Additionally, many synthetic fibers do not biodegrade, contributing to long-term environmental pollution.

Addressing the environmental impact of fashion requires a multi-faceted approach. Reducing water and chemical usage, minimizing waste, and promoting sustainable materials are essential steps. Consumers can play a crucial role by making more conscious choices, supporting eco-friendly brands, and advocating for better environmental practices in the industry.

8

Chapter 8: The Social Impact of Fashion

The fashion industry has a profound social impact, influencing the lives of millions of workers and communities worldwide. While the industry provides employment opportunities and economic growth, it is also plagued by issues such as labor exploitation, gender inequality, and unsafe working conditions. Addressing these social challenges is essential for creating a more just and equitable fashion landscape.

Labor exploitation is a pervasive issue in the fashion industry, particularly in developing countries. Garment workers, often women, face long hours, low wages, and poor working conditions. Many are employed in informal or precarious work arrangements, lacking job security and access to social protections. The pressure to meet tight production deadlines and cost-cutting measures often result in unsafe and unhealthy working environments. Ensuring fair wages, safe conditions, and labor rights for all workers is a critical step towards social justice in fashion.

Gender inequality is another significant concern. The majority of garment workers are women, yet they often face discrimination and limited opportunities for advancement. Gender-based violence and harassment are prevalent in some workplaces, further exacerbating the vulnerabilities of female workers. Empowering women through fair wages, education, and leadership opportunities can help address these disparities and promote gender equality in the industry.

The fashion industry also impacts local communities, both positively and negatively. On one hand, it provides employment and economic opportunities, particularly in regions with limited alternatives. On the other hand, the environmental degradation and resource depletion associated with production can harm local communities, affecting their health and livelihoods. Balancing the economic benefits of fashion with the need to protect and empower communities is crucial for sustainable development.

Consumers have a vital role to play in driving social change in fashion. By supporting ethical brands, demanding transparency, and advocating for better labor practices, we can contribute to a more equitable and humane industry. Our choices can help uplift workers, promote gender equality, and create a fashion landscape that values people as much as profit.

9

Chapter 9: The Intersection of Fashion and Culture

Fashion is deeply intertwined with culture, reflecting and shaping societal values, identities, and traditions. Throughout history, clothing has been used as a form of expression, communication, and resistance. Understanding the cultural significance of fashion can enrich our appreciation of its role in our lives and inspire more mindful and respectful choices.

Fashion often serves as a means of self-expression, allowing individuals to convey their identities, beliefs, and aspirations. From the bold styles of the 1960s counterculture to the subversive aesthetics of punk rock, clothing has been used to challenge norms and assert individuality. In contemporary society, fashion continues to be a powerful tool for self-expression, enabling people to navigate and negotiate their identities in a diverse and dynamic world.

Cultural traditions and heritage also play a significant role in fashion. Traditional garments and textiles carry rich histories and craftsmanship, often passed down through generations. These pieces reflect the values, aesthetics, and techniques of specific cultures, serving as a link between the past and the present. However, the appropriation of cultural elements by the fashion industry can lead to issues of exploitation and disrespect. It is essential to approach cultural fashion with sensitivity, acknowledging and honoring the origins and significance of these garments.

Fashion can also be a platform for social and political change. Throughout history, clothing has been used to make statements and advocate for causes. From the suffragette white dresses to the Black Panthers' iconic uniforms, fashion has been a powerful tool for activism and resistance. In recent years, movements such as sustainable fashion and body positivity have used clothing as a means to challenge industry norms and promote more inclusive and ethical practices.

By recognizing the cultural dimensions of fashion, we can make more informed and respectful choices. Celebrating diversity, honoring traditions, and using fashion as a platform for positive change can help create a more inclusive and meaningful fashion landscape.

10

Chapter 10: The Future of Sustainable Fashion

As the fashion industry grapples with its environmental and social impacts, there is a growing movement towards more sustainable and ethical practices. The future of fashion lies in embracing innovation, collaboration, and systemic change to create a more responsible and regenerative industry. This chapter explores some of the key trends and developments shaping the future of sustainable fashion.

One of the most promising trends is the rise of circular fashion. This approach emphasizes designing products for longevity, reuse, and recycling, creating a closed-loop system that minimizes waste and resource consumption. Brands are increasingly adopting circular principles, such as using recycled materials, designing for disassembly, and offering take-back programs. By creating products that can be easily repaired, repurposed, or recycled, the fashion industry can reduce its environmental footprint and promote a more sustainable model of consumption.

Collaboration and transparency are also crucial for driving change in the fashion industry. Brands, suppliers, and consumers must work together to create a more accountable and ethical supply chain. This involves sharing information about sourcing, production processes, and labor practices, enabling consumers to make informed decisions. Initiatives such as the

Fashion Transparency Index and the Sustainable Apparel Coalition are helping to promote greater transparency and accountability in the industry.

Innovation in materials and technology is another key area of focus. Advances in biofabrication, 3D printing, and sustainable textiles offer new opportunities for creating eco-friendly fashion. Researchers are developing materials that are biodegradable, renewable, and less resource-intensive, reducing the environmental impact of production. Additionally, technology can enhance the efficiency and sustainability of manufacturing processes, from waterless dyeing techniques to zero-waste pattern making.

Consumer education and advocacy are essential for driving demand for sustainable fashion. By raising awareness about the impacts of our fashion choices and promoting mindful consumption, we can create a culture that values quality, ethics, and sustainability. Initiatives such as Fashion Revolution Week and sustainable fashion influencers play a vital role in inspiring and mobilizing consumers to support ethical practices.

The future of sustainable fashion is bright, with endless possibilities for innovation and positive change. By embracing these trends and working together, we can create a fashion industry that is not only stylish but also sustainable and socially responsible.

11

Chapter 11: The Role of Policy and Regulation

Policy and regulation play a crucial role in shaping the fashion industry and promoting sustainable practices. Governments, international organizations, and industry bodies have the power to enforce standards, incentivize responsible behavior, and drive systemic change. This chapter explores the role of policy and regulation in creating a more ethical and sustainable fashion landscape.

Environmental regulations are essential for mitigating the fashion industry's impact on the planet. Policies that set limits on water usage, chemical pollution, and greenhouse gas emissions can help reduce the industry's environmental footprint. Governments can also promote sustainable practices through incentives such as tax breaks, subsidies, and grants for eco-friendly technologies and materials. By setting clear standards and providing support for innovation, policymakers can drive the transition towards a more sustainable fashion industry.

Labor rights and fair trade regulations are equally important for ensuring ethical practices in the fashion industry. Laws that protect workers' rights, such as fair wages, safe working conditions, and freedom of association, are critical for addressing labor exploitation. International agreements, such as the International Labour Organization's (ILO) conventions, set minimum standards for labor practices and provide a framework for enforcement. Governments can also support fair trade initiatives that ensure equitable treatment of workers and promote sustainable development in communities.

Transparency and accountability are key components of effective regulation. Policies that require brands to disclose information about their supply chains, sourcing practices, and environmental impact can help create a more accountable industry. Transparency initiatives, such as mandatory reporting and certification schemes, enable consumers to make informed decisions and hold brands accountable for their practices. By fostering a culture of transparency, policymakers can drive improvements in sustainability and ethics across the fashion industry.

Collaboration between governments, industry bodies, and civil society is essential for creating effective policy and regulation. Multi-stakeholder initiatives, such as the Sustainable Apparel Coalition and the United Nations' Fashion Industry Charter for Climate Action, bring together diverse actors to develop and implement sustainable solutions. By working together, these stakeholders can address the complex challenges of the fashion industry and create a more sustainable and just future.

Policy and regulation have a vital role to play in transforming the fashion industry. By setting standards, promoting transparency, and incentivizing responsible behavior, governments and organizations can drive meaningful change and create a more sustainable and ethical fashion landscape.

12

Chapter 12: The Ethical Consumer

The ethical consumer is a key driver of change in the fashion industry. By making informed and conscious choices, consumers can support ethical practices, reduce their environmental impact, and promote a more sustainable fashion ecosystem. This chapter explores the characteristics and actions of an ethical consumer and how individuals can contribute to positive change.

An ethical consumer prioritizes transparency and accountability in their purchasing decisions. They seek out brands that provide detailed information about their sourcing, production processes, and labor practices. Ethical consumers value honesty and integrity, supporting companies that are committed to ethical and sustainable practices. By demanding transparency, they encourage brands to adopt more responsible behaviors and foster a culture of accountability.

Sustainability is a core principle for ethical consumers. They prioritize eco-friendly materials, such as organic cotton, bamboo, and recycled fibers, and seek out garments that are designed to last. Ethical consumers also embrace practices such as second-hand shopping, clothing swaps, and rental services, reducing the demand for new products and minimizing waste. By making sustainable choices, they contribute to a more circular and regenerative fashion system.

Fair labor practices are another important consideration for ethical consumers. They support brands that ensure fair wages, safe working conditions, and labor rights for garment workers. Ethical consumers are aware of the human cost of fashion and seek to uplift workers by choosing fair trade and ethically produced garments. They also advocate for better labor practices and hold brands accountable for their treatment of workers.

Mindful consumption is a defining characteristic of an ethical consumer. They approach fashion with intention and purpose, avoiding impulse purchases and prioritizing quality over quantity. Ethical consumers invest in timeless, versatile pieces that reflect their personal style and can be worn for years. They also care for their garments, extending their lifespan through proper maintenance and repair.

The ethical consumer is a powerful force for change in the fashion industry. By making conscious choices and supporting responsible practices, individuals can drive demand for sustainable and ethical fashion. Together, ethical consumers can create a more just and compassionate fashion landscape, benefiting both people and the planet.

13

Chapter 13: The Impact of COVID-19 on the Fashion Industry

The COVID-19 pandemic has had a profound impact on the fashion industry, disrupting supply chains, altering consumer behavior, and highlighting the vulnerabilities of the global fashion system. This chapter explores the challenges and opportunities presented by the pandemic and how the industry can emerge more resilient and sustainable.

The pandemic exposed the fragility of global supply chains, with factory closures, shipping delays, and workforce shortages affecting production and distribution. Many garment workers faced job losses and reduced incomes, exacerbating existing vulnerabilities. The crisis underscored the need for more resilient and equitable supply chains that prioritize worker well-being and fair labor practices.

Consumer behavior also shifted significantly during the pandemic. With lockdowns and social distancing measures in place, demand for fashion declined, and many consumers reevaluated their purchasing habits. The pandemic accelerated the adoption of digital channels, with online shopping and virtual fashion experiences becoming more prominent. This shift presents an opportunity for brands to engage with consumers in new ways and promote sustainable and ethical practices.

The pandemic also brought renewed attention to the environmental impact of fashion. With reduced industrial activity, there was a temporary decline in pollution and emissions, highlighting the need for more sustainable practices. Many consumers became more conscious of their environmental footprint and sought out eco-friendly alternatives. This shift in awareness and behavior can drive demand for sustainable fashion and encourage brands to adopt greener practices.

The fashion industry has an opportunity to emerge from the pandemic stronger and more sustainable. By prioritizing resilience, equity, and sustainability, brands can build a more responsible and compassionate industry. This includes adopting circular fashion principles, investing in innovative materials and technologies, and fostering transparency and accountability. Collaboration and collective action are essential for driving systemic change and creating a fashion ecosystem that benefits both people and the planet.

The COVID-19 pandemic has been a wake-up call for the fashion industry, revealing its vulnerabilities and highlighting the need for change. By embracing the lessons learned and seizing the opportunities for transformation, the industry can create a more sustainable and equitable future.

14

Chapter 14: The Role of Education in Sustainable Fashion

Education is a powerful tool for promoting sustainable fashion practices and fostering a more conscious consumer culture. By raising awareness about the environmental and social impacts of fashion, we can empower individuals to make informed choices and advocate for positive change. This chapter explores the role of education in driving sustainability in the fashion industry.

Incorporating sustainability into fashion education programs is essential for preparing the next generation of designers, marketers, and consumers. Fashion schools and universities can integrate courses on sustainable materials, ethical production, and circular fashion principles into their curricula. By equipping students with the knowledge and skills to create eco-friendly and socially responsible fashion, we can cultivate a new wave of industry leaders who prioritize sustainability.

Public awareness campaigns and educational initiatives can also play a significant role in promoting sustainable fashion. Organizations, NGOs, and influencers can use various platforms to share information about the impacts of fashion and the importance of ethical practices. Social media, documentaries, workshops, and community events are effective ways to engage the public and inspire them to take action. By making sustainability a mainstream topic, we can encourage more people to adopt mindful consumption habits.

Consumer education is crucial for driving demand for sustainable fashion. Providing information about the environmental and social impacts of different materials, production processes, and brands can help consumers make more informed choices. Labels, certifications, and transparency initiatives can guide consumers in identifying ethical and eco-friendly products. By educating consumers about the benefits of sustainable fashion, we can shift market demand towards more responsible practices.

Education also plays a role in fostering a culture of repair and reuse. Teaching basic sewing and mending skills can empower individuals to extend the life of their garments and reduce waste. DIY fashion workshops and online tutorials can inspire creativity and encourage people to repurpose and customize their clothing. By promoting a mindset of resourcefulness and care, education can help reduce the throwaway culture associated with fast fashion.

The role of education in sustainable fashion cannot be overstated. By raising awareness, equipping individuals with knowledge, and fostering a culture of responsibility, education can drive meaningful change in the fashion industry. Together, we can create a more informed, conscious, and sustainable fashion ecosystem.

15

Chapter 15: The Influence of Social Media on Fashion

Social media has revolutionized the fashion industry, transforming how trends are set, brands are marketed, and consumers engage with fashion. While social media has democratized fashion and provided a platform for diverse voices, it has also contributed to the rapid consumption and disposal of clothing. This chapter explores the dual influence of social media on fashion and how it can be harnessed to promote sustainability.

Social media platforms, such as Instagram, TikTok, and Pinterest, have made fashion more accessible and inclusive. Influencers, bloggers, and everyday users can share their styles and inspire millions of followers, breaking down traditional barriers in the fashion industry. This democratization has allowed for a wider range of voices and styles to be represented, challenging conventional beauty standards and promoting diversity.

However, the fast-paced nature of social media can also contribute to the throwaway culture of fashion. The constant stream of new trends and styles can create pressure to constantly update wardrobes and purchase new items. Influencers often collaborate with fast fashion brands, promoting inexpensive and trendy pieces that encourage rapid consumption. This cycle of overconsumption has significant environmental and social impacts, exacerbating the problems associated with fast fashion.

Despite these challenges, social media also has the potential to drive positive change in the fashion industry. Influencers and brands that prioritize sustainability can use their platforms to raise awareness about ethical practices and promote eco-friendly alternatives. By sharing information about sustainable materials, fair labor practices, and responsible consumption, they can inspire their followers to make more conscious choices. Campaigns such as #FashionRevolution and #SecondHandSeptember have harnessed the power of social media to advocate for transparency, sustainability, and second-hand shopping.

User-generated content and online communities can also promote sustainable fashion. Fashion enthusiasts can share their tips on clothing care, DIY projects, and thrift shopping, creating a culture of resourcefulness and creativity. Social media challenges and hashtags can encourage users to showcase their sustainable fashion choices and inspire others to follow suit. By leveraging the influence of social media, we can amplify the message of sustainability and create a more conscious and responsible fashion community.

Social media's influence on fashion is undeniable, and it can be a powerful tool for promoting sustainability. By harnessing the reach and engagement of these platforms, we can drive positive change, raise awareness, and inspire a more ethical and eco-friendly approach to fashion.

16

Chapter 16: Building a Sustainable Fashion Brand

Building a sustainable fashion brand involves a commitment to ethical practices, environmental responsibility, and transparency. This chapter explores the key principles and steps for creating a sustainable fashion brand that prioritizes people and the planet.

1. **Ethical Sourcing**: Sustainable fashion brands prioritize ethical sourcing by selecting materials and suppliers that adhere to fair labor practices and environmental standards. This involves choosing organic, recycled, or renewable materials and working with suppliers who ensure safe working conditions and fair wages for their workers. Transparency in the supply chain is crucial for building trust with consumers and demonstrating a commitment to ethical practices.
2. **Eco-Friendly Production**: Sustainable brands minimize their environmental impact by adopting eco-friendly production methods. This includes reducing water and energy usage, minimizing waste, and using non-toxic dyes and finishes. Brands can also explore innovative production techniques, such as 3D printing and zero-waste pattern making, to further reduce their environmental footprint. Investing in sustainable technology and practices can create a more efficient and

responsible production process.

3. **Design for Longevity**: Creating durable and timeless designs is a key principle of sustainable fashion. Brands should focus on quality craftsmanship and versatile styles that can withstand changing trends. Designing for longevity involves choosing durable materials, reinforcing garment construction, and offering repair services. By creating products that are built to last, brands can reduce the frequency of replacements and promote a more sustainable approach to fashion.

4. **Circular Fashion**: Embracing circular fashion principles can help brands reduce waste and extend the lifecycle of their products. This involves designing garments that can be easily repaired, repurposed, or recycled. Brands can offer take-back programs, where consumers can return their used garments for recycling or resale. Additionally, collaborating with second-hand marketplaces and rental services can create a circular economy that keeps clothing in use for longer.

5. **Transparency and Accountability**: Building a sustainable fashion brand requires a commitment to transparency and accountability. Brands should provide detailed information about their sourcing, production processes, and environmental impact. This can be achieved through certifications, reporting, and engaging with consumers through social media and other platforms. By being open and honest about their practices, brands can build trust and credibility with their customers.

6. **Consumer Education**: Sustainable fashion brands play a vital role in educating consumers about the importance of ethical and eco-friendly practices. This involves sharing information about the impacts of fashion, providing tips on garment care and repair, and encouraging mindful consumption. By fostering a culture of awareness and responsibility, brands can inspire their customers to make more conscious choices.

Building a sustainable fashion brand is a journey that requires dedication, innovation, and collaboration. By prioritizing ethical practices, environmental responsibility, and transparency, brands can create a positive impact and contribute to a more sustainable and ethical fashion industry.

17

Chapter 17: The Journey Towards an Ethical Wardrobe

The journey towards an ethical wardrobe is a personal and ongoing process that involves making conscious and informed choices. This final chapter provides practical tips and strategies for building a sustainable and ethical wardrobe that reflects your values and style.

1. **Assess Your Current Wardrobe**: Begin by taking stock of your existing clothing. Identify the pieces you love and wear frequently, as well as those that no longer serve you. This process can help you understand your style preferences and identify gaps in your wardrobe. Consider donating, selling, or recycling items you no longer need, and focus on building a collection of versatile and timeless pieces.
2. **Prioritize Quality Over Quantity**: When adding new pieces to your wardrobe, prioritize quality over quantity. Invest in well-made garments that are designed to last and can be worn in multiple ways. Look for durable materials and high-quality craftsmanship, and choose timeless styles that transcend seasonal trends. By opting for quality, you can reduce the frequency of replacements and create a more sustainable wardrobe.
3. **Support Ethical and Sustainable Brands**: Research and support

brands that prioritize ethical and sustainable practices. Look for certifications such as Fair Trade, GOTS (Global Organic Textile Standard), and B Corp that indicate a commitment to responsible production. Transparency and accountability are key indicators of an ethical brand, so seek out companies that provide detailed information about their sourcing and production processes.

4. **Embrace Second-Hand and Vintage**: Thrift stores, consignment shops, and online marketplaces offer a wealth of pre-loved garments that are often unique and high-quality. Embracing second-hand shopping reduces the demand for new products and minimizes waste. Additionally, vintage pieces add character and history to your wardrobe, allowing you to express your individuality while making a sustainable choice.

5. **Learn Basic Sewing and Repair Skills**: Extending the life of your garments is a crucial aspect of building an ethical wardrobe. Learning basic sewing and repair skills can empower you to fix minor issues and customize your clothing. Simple tasks such as sewing on buttons, mending tears, and hemming can keep your garments in good condition and reduce the need for replacements.

6. **Mindful Consumption**: Approach fashion with intention and mindfulness. Avoid impulse purchases and take the time to consider whether a new item aligns with your style and values. Focus on building a wardrobe that reflects your personality and lifestyle, and make choices that prioritize sustainability and ethics. Mindful consumption involves making deliberate and thoughtful decisions, rather than succumbing to the pressures of fast fashion.

The journey towards an ethical wardrobe is a rewarding and transformative process that benefits both you and the planet. By making conscious choices and prioritizing sustainability, you can create a wardrobe

Description:
" The Ethical Wardrobe: How Fashion Can Save the Planet and Our Conscience" is a thought-provoking journey into the world of sustainable

CHAPTER 17: THE JOURNEY TOWARDS AN ETHICAL WARDROBE

fashion, written with heart and depth. This book dives into the fast-paced, glamorous façade of the fashion industry to reveal the environmental and social costs hidden beneath. It's a call to action for consumers to rethink their fashion choices, offering insights into how our clothing habits can be transformed for the betterment of the planet and society.

Through 17 engaging chapters, the book covers various aspects of ethical fashion, from the devastating impact of fast fashion to the innovative solutions paving the way for a more sustainable future. It highlights the power of consumer choice, the importance of supporting ethical brands, and the role of technology and policy in driving change. The narrative weaves together real-world examples, industry insights, and practical tips, making it an essential guide for anyone looking to build a more responsible wardrobe.

By the end of this book, readers will feel empowered to make informed decisions that align with their values, embrace slow fashion, and contribute to a more just and compassionate fashion industry. "The Ethical Wardrobe" is not just about clothes—it's about making a positive impact on the world through the choices we make every day.

www.ingramcontent.com/pod-product-compliance
Lightning Source LLC
LaVergne TN
LVHW020458080526
838202LV00057B/6032